How to Get Rich during a Recession

Ways on How to Take Advantage of the Economic Downturn to Build Your Wealth

By: Samantha Lee Bernard

9781681279497

PUBLISHERS NOTES

Disclaimer – Speedy Publishing LLC

This publication is intended to provide helpful and informative material. It is not intended to diagnose, treat, cure, or prevent any health problem or condition, nor is intended to replace the advice of a physician. No action should be taken solely on the contents of this book. Always consult your physician or qualified health-care professional on any matters regarding your health and before adopting any suggestions in this book or drawing inferences from it.

The author and publisher specifically disclaim all responsibility for any liability, loss or risk, personal or otherwise, which is incurred as a consequence, directly or indirectly, from the use or application of any contents of this book.

Any and all product names referenced within this book are the trademarks of their respective owners. None of these owners have sponsored, authorized, endorsed, or approved this book.

Always read all information provided by the manufacturers' product labels before using their products. The author and publisher are not responsible for claims made by manufacturers.

This book was originally printed before 2014. This is an adapted reprint by Speedy Publishing LLC with newly updated content designed to help readers with much more accurate and timely information and data.

Speedy Publishing LLC

40 E Main Street, Newark, Delaware, 19711

Contact Us: 1-888-248-4521

Website: http://www.speedypublishing.co

REPRINTED Paperback Edition: 9781681279497:

Manufactured in the United States of America

DEDICATION

This book is dedicated to my sister, Jonah. You are a determined business woman and I admire you for that. Thanks for coming to my rescue whenever I need you.

TABLE OF CONTENTS

Chapter 1- Why the Recession Shouldn't Scare You 5

Chapter 2- The Major Players of the US Economy 10

Chapter 3- How Employees Can Be Recession-Proof 25

Chapter 4- Recession-Proofing Your Business 36

Chapter 5- Unbelievable Benefits of Recession 45

Chapter 6 – How to Build Wealth in a Failing Economy 48

About The Author 58

Chapter 1- Why the Recession Shouldn't Scare You

If there's one thing that can be said to symbolize today's society, it is the expectation of instant gratification. We want what we want, and we want it now. We have cars that drive over two hundred miles per hour, jets that break the sound barrier and rockets that go into outer space. We are constantly expanding our horizons, stretching our capabilities beyond the bounds of human comprehension, and pushing into unknown territory with each breath we take.

It's never occurred to us that we're not intended to do most of the things we do in the name of progress. If you had asked our ancestors two hundred years ago if we would ever go into space, they would have told you that if God had intended for us to fly he'd have given us wings. Yet here we are. We've accomplished the impossible, and rather than being satisfied with that we push ourselves harder to accomplish the impossible faster and more spectacularly than ever before.

Fast food, microwaves, mail order videos and payday loans have encouraged us to think as far ahead as the next forty eight hours when it comes to our goals and expectations. We're lured, tempted and taunted by promises of overnight riches on the Internet with almost no work at all, and we've long since lost our appreciation for the toil and frustration of hard labor in favor of replaced those outdated methods of getting things done with updated technology that can accomplish the same thing in half the amount of time.

We live in a now society, which is why economic recessions are so difficult for us to accept. If we have a limited amount of capital coming and going, and a limited amount of growth happening in industries all across the world, we can't accomplish our goals in a short amount of time. We might even have to set those goals aside in favor of meeting our short term needs, such as keeping food on the table, or the long term, like building our retirement savings. Without booming enterprise we can't live the American dream and start our own business, because we need to provide our family with the security that the daily grind provides-and with millions of people across the country getting laid off every day, we're just happy to have a job.

What many people fail to understand is that economic recession is simply a normal part of the regular cycle of the business world. Although some recessions are more dramatic than others, the bottom line is that economic recessions happen regularly. If we didn't have economic recessions from time to time to the business world would be in trouble. Economic recessions:

- Cull out businesses that aren't going to survive the long haul. If you look at any guide to surviving an economic recession they'll tell you that the most important thing to do is to either work for or run a company that's going to continue to thrive even in the face of economic recession. Apple, IBM and Microsoft aren't going anywhere, no matter how ugly the recession gets. Companies that provide basic needs like electric and food will always be in demand, because they have a product that is always going to have a need.

- Wipe scams off the market. When economic recessions first begin they provide an atmosphere for get-rich-scams to thrive because people are desperate to break free of the sharp constrictions on their income that the recession and the accompanying consequences, as the recession drags on people are going to be too busy pumping their income into legitimate businesses trying to keep their heads above water to keep these frauds afloat. Sooner or later they're going to have to get a real job.

- Force the government to tighten the strings on its budget. It's one thing to be able to spend exorbitantly when taxpayers can afford the inflation that goes along with it, but when taxpayers have to start counting their pennies the government has to tighten its belt right along with them and start funneling the funds that it has coming in into productive programs that are going to do more than suck resources.

- Drive down prices. Without economic recessions there would be nothing driving down the price of goods and services, and our inflation would be even more ridiculous than it already is. When goods aren't selling, companies have to drive their prices down to make them more appealing or they will completely lose their investment-and they hate doing that.

How to Get Rich during a Recession

Throughout history there have been many, many instances of economic recession. Think about the Great Depression back in the '30s. For two years in the early '80s there was a recession, and July 1990-March 1991 and November 2001-November 2002 were classified as economic recessions as well. Some of these periods inspired a tighter pinch on the pocketbooks of American citizens than others, but they happened.

After each of these recessions, came periods of economic growth that allowed companies to get back on their feet and the economy to start flowing again as families had more money to spend. Economic recessions are nothing new. It's how we deal with them that determine the effect they're going to have on our economy.

The Biblical Roots of Modern-Day Recession

Did you know that economic recession is actually ordered in the Bible? Every 49 years the people of Israel were ordered to celebrate a year of Jubilee, where the land would lie fallow and all property would be returned to its original owner. This year and the following year there would be no new crops, so the people were required to prepare. Imagine: Every 50 years they Israelites knew there was going to be an economic recession.

If you could predict when an economic recession would occur, what would you do? Would you just step back and allow it to happen, or do you think that you would take steps to prepare yourself and your company to weather the storm? Do you think you might even study the trends and find a way to make that economic recession work for you? Maybe store away a little bit extra during those forty nine years so that you could see to the people who didn't have the foresight to put away what they needed to get by those two years of famine?

Samantha Lee Bernard
That's what we're going to be discussing in the next couple of sections. What you need to do to help yourself ride out a recession without losing everything you've worked so hard for, and what you can do to make this recession work for you. Remember, recession is nothing new. Men and women have been surviving recessions for as long as there has been an economy to recede.

The question is what are you going to do about it?

Chapter 2 - The Major Players of the US Economy

When people think about an economic recession the first thought that comes to mind is, "What am I going to do?" Their primary concern is for how they are going to be able to meet their financial obligations with the economy slipping steadily away.

That's a legitimate concern, and one that symbolizes a sense of responsibility. Unfortunately, there are some ugly side effects to economic recessions. Companies have to trim the fat in order to ride out the fact that consumers are plugging less and less money into their business, and usually that fat comes in the form of non-essential personnel. In other words, if you aren't on their list of most needed people your job will be the first to go when they're looking for a way to cut back.

They can always replace you when things start picking back up.

You wouldn't be human if you weren't a little concerned with how you're going to pay your bills in the face of an economic recession.

Samantha Lee Bernard
The good news is that if you know the steps to take to protect your job and your company you can minimize the damage when it all hits the fan. As a matter of fact, with a little bit of effort and some savvy investing that would put the rookies on Wall Street to shame you can do much more than minimize the damage.

You can make the recession work for you.

Real Estate

Considering the fact that it was real estate that started the ball rolling toward economic disaster in the first place, it's rather ironic that it is in real estate that investors really have the opportunity to capitalize on economic recession and turn what could be a potentially devastating economic downturn into a major opportunity for profit. Why? Because real estate is one of the major assets whose value is plummeting in the face of a never ending stream of foreclosures and bankruptcies, and it is real estate whose value is guaranteed to go up when the recession is over.

Think about it. Will there ever come a time when real estate isn't a desperately needed asset? Absolutely not! People are always going to need places to live and place to work, and because of that there will always be a need for real estate. That's why a huge percentage of entrepreneurs are jumping on board the real estate bandwagon to grow wealth and increase their net worth. It's one of the only markets out there that's guaranteed to never become obsolete!

A major contributor to the current economic crises and the fact that major players like Freddie Mac and Fannie Mae are going under is the huge number of people defaulting on their mortgages. When the concept of interest only loans and other special programs designed to help those individuals who otherwise would

How to Get Rich during a Recession

never qualify for any type of mortgage purchase a home first came out everyone thought it was a great idea-and in many ways it was. It placed the power to purchase property in the hands of people who otherwise wouldn't have the ability to do it, and it sent banks into raptures as more and more people came to them for assistance in buying or refinancing their first home.

Then reality struck. The bottom line is that many of these homeowners weren't able to get a mortgage in the first place because they didn't have the means to repay it, and while for some people the programs worked like they were supposed to (interest only loans for first time homebuyers still trying to find their niche in the workplace, for example, who later became responsible citizens and were able to shoulder the increased burden of their mortgage payment when the time came to begin making payments on the principle) others just found themselves going farther and farther into debt.

Skip ahead six months to a year, and suddenly a huge percentage of these homeowners are defaulting on their loans. Banks are foreclosing left and right, and they're struggling to get rid of these properties as quickly as possible to get them off their records. Each property goes to a foreclosure auction, where it sells for less than it would have outright at fair market value, and the bank barely reclaims its investment.

Fast forward a little farther and suddenly a large number of people are out of jobs as the economy continues to slide. You have a huge pool of homeowners whose income, once strong and steady courtesy of major manufacturers and/or the United States government is now no longer sufficient to meet their financial obligations. They can't pay their mortgages that they took out when their resources were more than sufficient to meet their needs, and the bank has to foreclose on those properties as well.

Samantha Lee Bernard

The real estate market is plunged into chaos, property values are falling rapidly in an attempt to stem the tide of destruction sweeping from coast to coast, and clever investors are rubbing their hands together in glee.

During an economic recession homebuyers simply aren't buying homes. They're pumping their money into other things. This inspires desperate homeowners to put their homes on the market for far less than they're actually worth in an attempt to make a sale that will be adequate to allow them to pay off the bank and be free of the mortgage default hanging over their head.

Enter the real estate investor. They soothingly placate the homeowner, assuring them that of course they're there to put everything to right. They contact the bank to let them know that they will be purchasing the property so that the bank can halt any legal foreclosure proceedings they may have initiated, and then they pay the happy homeowner and send them on their way, holding the deed to the property.

This process is repeated over and over again every day during an economic recession, particularly once that recession has begun to have a positive (or negative, depending on how you want to look at it) effect on the value of the housing market. It's not at all unusual for a clever investor to find a homeowner who has built up some equity in their home and who will gladly sell it for a fraction of the cost it would go for on the open market.

In dollars and cents, it means that it's not at all unheard of for an investor to purchase a $350,000 home for under $200,000 during an economic recession. The value of the property has fallen so far and the homeowner is so far behind on their financial obligations that they are willing to let the property go for a song just to dodge the stigma of bankruptcy or foreclosure that would otherwise be lingering over their heads.

After the investor has the property in his hands he has a choice. He can either choose to turn right around and sell it to a rehabber or private homeowner. He can hold on to it, rehab it himself and rent it out (since affordable rental property will be highly in demand in the face of the rapidly failing housing market, with hundreds of families ousted from their homes and left to find another place to live), or simply sit and hold on to it.

As an investor during an economic recession it's vitally important that you understand the basic framework of a recession. THE RECESSION IS NOT GOING TO LAST FOREVER! Sooner or later the economy is going to start getting back to normal, and when it does the value on your investment is going to rise back up. That $200,000 home is suddenly going to sell for $350,000 again-more if it happens to be in an area that sees a tremendous boom as a result of the ending depression.

That means that if you can afford to do it, the best thing you can do at this point is play a waiting game. You know the value of your property is only going to rise, and if you rehab it while you're waiting you can watch the value rise even more. Let's take that $350,000 house and use it for an example again. Let's assume for a moment that the house is sitting on a lightly wooded lot with a big backyard an easy commute away from a major, booming industrial area.

Let's also assume that the industrial area saw a major boom as a result of the ending recession, and that because of that boom property values in the area were jerked back up. That house that was worth $350,000 and sold for $200,000 is suddenly worth $400,000; however, while they were waiting for the end of the recession the homeowner also took the opportunity to rehab the property, doing some landscaping, adding a pool and a spa room and installing all new plumbing and appliances.

Suddenly that property that the investor bought for $200,000 and invested $40,000 to fix up is worth over $500,000. Even with the additional $40,000 investment for the rehabilitation the real estate purchaser is going to walk away with a tidy $100,000 in their pocket-more than many executives make in two years, and all because they were clever enough to take advantage of an opportunity when one presented itself on the back of an economic recession.

If you're looking for a way to take advantage of the recession and you have the time and the money to do it, I strongly recommend real estate. The good thing about real estate is that if you know the ins and outs of the business you can enjoy a return from this career whether you choose to think in the short term or the long term-although, for the sake of this book, I'm going to encourage you to put at least a little bit of thought into the long term.

Remember, long term when you're talking about an economic recession isn't the same as when you're talking about the long term anywhere else. A recession usually lasts less than a year. A year's worth of stockpiling for a lifetime's worth of profit. Hmmm...

What to Look for When You're Buying Real Estate

When you're going shopping for real estate in the middle of an economic recession you can pretty much guarantee that whatever you purchase, you're going to be able to make a profit. There are certain parts of the country that take a little longer to be affected when a recession strikes, but sooner or later every place is going to start to feel the pinch-which means you can basically stick a pin in the map when you're trying to decide where you want to make your investment.

Of course, just because you can make a profit just about anywhere doesn't mean that you shouldn't take measures to maximize that profit. If you were sitting in the middle of a giant room of sweets that were yours for the taking absolutely free, would you go for the Godiva chocolate or the M&Ms? When you have the choice between a property that you're going to make a minimal investment on and a property that you will make an incredible profit on when the economy starts rising up again, go for the property that's going to bring you the best return!

Where are you going to find the best deals? Urban properties and homes in the suburbs of these urban areas are always more highly in demand than those that require a lengthy commute to get to life's essentials. Homes in the suburbs of Washington, D.C. are going to sell for a greater profit (and much more quickly) than a home in a small town like Rexville, NY. (Don't worry if you've never heard of it-most of the rest of the world have not either!)

When you first begin investing it's usually recommended that you pick a property close to home, where you know the neighborhood, the general ambiance and, most importantly, what sells! If you choose to do your own rehab this is particularly important, as there are many areas in the country that are particularly prized for their historical value and which will bring a much lower return on your investment if they've been stripped and decked out in the latest style than if they'd been carefully restored. An experienced rehabber will know this. A beginning investor will not.

Other factors you may want to take into consideration before closing the deal are:

- The quality of the neighborhood. Unfortunately, all urban areas have their slums. An area with a high crime rate, a wide-spread amount of graffiti and property damage, regular drug activity and daily visits from the police is going to be much less desirable to a prospective buyer than a home situation in a nicer part of town, where they can safely allow their children to step out the front door without having to worry that they won't come home.

- The condition of the house. There have been many, many investors that have plunged right in to the world of real estate and rehabilitation and bought a handyman's special only to discover that by the time they got done paying for the repairs to the property the profit margin was considerably less than what they were hoping for-and what they would have made investing in a property that needed a little less work.

- Before you commit to buying a property, take the time to have the home inspected carefully. Certain factors, such as a leaky roof, faulty foundation, termites and extensive mold, are going to be both difficult and expensive to fix. Unless you can quite literally get the property for a song, justifying the amount of time and expense you're going to put into the restoration project, it may be best to allow that one to pass you by.

- What you plan to do with it afterwards.

This is probably the biggest factor when it comes to real estate investing, because what you plan to do with the property after you purchase it makes all the difference when you're determining what types of properties are suitable and what are not. If you're planning on rehabilitating a property, then reselling it as a single family residence, purchasing a small ranch house on the edge of the city may be a perfectly profitable proposition.

How to Get Rich during a Recession

You'll likely be able to sell the property for more than you paid for it and justify the investment.

On the other hand, if you're planning on renting the property out you're going to want to investigate the current rental rates of the neighborhood before you'll be able to determine the success of the investment with any degree of accuracy. There are some areas where income based housing drives the average rental price of the neighborhood down, which is good news for renters but could result in major inconvenience for the investor who has paid hundreds of thousands of dollars for a property that they are only going to be able to rent for a couple hundred dollars a month.

The moral of our story? Take the time to carefully consider your options and do your homework before closing the deal, no matter how appealing that deal may be.

Of course, if you've been investing in real estate for the past ten years none of this is news to you! Experienced investors who are familiar with things like market trends and identifying weaknesses in potential properties will find the buffet of low priced real estate spread out before them a tempting proposition, and reaching beyond their immediate demographic boundaries may offer a new wealth of possibilities for tremendous profit gain.

Just remember that investing during a recession is a slightly different proposition than investing when the economy is booming. You're going to hear me say this over and over again; because it can't be emphasized enough-when you're investing in real estate during a recession you're investing in the long term. Many of today's real estate investors have made their fortune in the market by taking advantage of today's "Now, now, now!" mindset and investing in and disposing of real estate in a very brief amount of time. When the economy is strong it's not at all unusual for an experienced investor to be able to purchase and flip a property within the space of week-experienced rehabbers in a month of less. Any property that you invest in during a recession may remain in your possession for several months before you are able to realize a maximum return, because the whole point of investing during a recession is to purchase an asset at the lowest price possible and sell it when the economy goes back up.

It's rare for the experienced investor to find themselves in this situation, but it's entirely possible to spread yourself too thin when the temptation of pages upon pages of available property was just too much to resist. Suddenly they're responsible not only for the amount they've paid for the initial investment to purchase the property in the first place, but for the taxes, rehabilitation and maintenance required to keep it maintained and prepare it for sale.

Try to limit yourself with a realistic expectation of what you can afford in the long term. If as the recession continues you find you have more than enough capital in hand to pick up a couple more properties you always have that option, but disposing of a property you can no longer afford during a recession can be more difficult than taking a submarine and going diving for Atlantis-which is the reason that investing in real estate during a recession is so lucrative to begin with.

Stock Market Investments

As businesses begin to lose money and booming, raging profits give way to something a little more on par with their daily expenses the door to successfully investing in the market swings wide open and invites you in. The principles of investing in the stock market during a recession are remarkably similar to the principles of investing in real estate. When you invest in the stock market during a recession

How to Get Rich during a Recession

you have the opportunity to take advantage of a company's poor fortune.

How? When companies are making money hand over fist the value of the company goes through the roof, and as the value of the company raises so too does the value of its stock. So when a company is riding high the price of the stock is going to be high as well. Shift the situation a bit, however, and the story changes.

Take mortgage giant Fannie Mae. In the month of July 2008 alone the value of its stock fell from $16 and change to a little over $8 a share. By September of that same year the share price was under a dollar courtesy of the sheer quantity of its borrowers that had defaulted on their loans.

Fannie Mae is only one of many companies who suffered a similar fate during the last recession. It's situations like these that present stock holders willing to think in the long term with a golden opportunity to make a profit. If they can purchase the shares when they are low, as in Fannie Mae's case, less than 1/16 their value, they can sit back, fold their hands and wait for the recession to end. When the recession has ended they can sell their shares for a tidy profit, sit back and pat themselves on the back for a job well done.

That doesn't mean you should go out, find a company that's failing and throw your life savings into their stock. That's a recipe for disaster that many investors have fallen into over the years! This is a golden opportunity that definitely shouldn't be allowed to pass you by, but there are a few things you should watch out for.

1) First and foremost, when you're choosing a company to invest in it's essential that you choose one that's going to weather the storm of the recession and bounce back when the time comes. If

you sink your savings into a company and it goes under as a result of the recession you're going to be no better off than you were before. To determine whether or not a company will survive to see a bright new future rather than being culled out when the recession separates the wheat from the chaff, answer the following questions:

- How long have they been in business? Companies that have been in business for many years are unlikely to go under because of a simple recession-in fact; they've likely weathered many of them in their time. A company that's already proven their staying power is an excellent choice of investment, and should definitely be given first consideration.

- What do they do? Although companies that specialize tend to be movers and shakers when the economy is normal, if they are unable to expand and "macro" themselves (a topic we'll talk about in greater detail in just a bit) to adjust to the changing economy they're going to go under. If a company has not been able to expand and diversify, and if it doesn't offer a product that people are guaranteed to need day after day and therefore are pretty much guaranteed to keep coming back for, it's at a high risk for going under during the recession and should be given a wide berth.

- Is their industry stable? Historically, there are certain industries that tend to fare better in a recession than others, and these should be given firm consideration when you're expanding your portfolio. Utility stocks (telephone, electric, gas), food and "escapes" such as cigarettes, alcohol and gambling have a history of tremendous success when it comes to riding out a recession because these are the industries that most consumers deem necessities and will continue pumping their money into.

How to Get Rich during a Recession

- Is it a necessity? The industries listed above are stable choices during a recession because they are deemed to be necessities; however, if there is one industry that you can be sure is not going to go anywhere in the face of any kind of recession, it is the healthcare and pharmaceutical industry. Regardless of what the economy looks like, people are going to get sick and they're going to need their medication to recover. This is a strong, stable choice for your portfolio, and it's one that you can count on to bring in a steady, if not always remarkable, return.

- What about gold? Gold isn't going anywhere. If you're looking for a safe, solid and low risk investment during a recession period, gold is an excellent choice. There is very little chance that the value of gold is going to depreciate rapidly, and it's definitely not going anywhere.

- Successful investing isn't always just a matter of knowing what to invest in. Many times, it's also a matter of knowing what not to invest in. There are certain industries that often bring about good returns when the stock market is high, but who are extremely risky during times of recession. Can you guess which industries those are? Right. Any industry that specializes in luxury services is going to take a hit when conscientious investors start counting their pennies, and as a result so are their stockholders. Good industries to avoid include airlines, luxury resorts, restaurants (unless they have been around for a while) and, of course, financial and lending institutions (who are likely to go under as their borrowers slip further and further into debt).

- If you aren't familiar with the process of investing the best thing you could do for yourself to ensure the continued growth and success of your investments is find a skilled financial counselor and/or investment broker to work with. Ideally, they'll be able to look at a company's past history and their current place on the market and let you know whether or not they are a good choice for investment. Choose your broker with care, however; the last thing you want is to see your hard work and cautious planning fall apart because your broker was overly ambitious and pushed you into an investment that was doomed to failure from the very beginning.

2) Diversify. Regardless of how established a company is, there's no way to positively predict how they are going to react in the event of a recession. Your mother always told you not to put all of your eggs in a single basket, and she was absolutely right. If you can spread your investments around a bit through several companies in a variety of industries you will stand a better chance of being able to profit from this recession. Even if the bottom falls out of one and it goes under as a result of the poor economy you will have the others to fall back on and ensure that you are never left holding absolutely nothing at the end of the day.

Like real estate, investing in stocks now opens the door to the possibility of tremendous profits down the road. You may not be able to enjoy the same $100,000 gain you would have had you chosen to invest in houses rather than stocks, but you will enjoy a comfortable profit that will help carry you through on into the new economy.

Picture this. Let's say that you decided to take advantage of Fannie Mae's current position and bout 4,000 shares of stock. (For the record, this is not something I recommend; Fannie Mae is simply a hypothetical example for the purpose of this book). At a dollar each, you'd be able to acquire the stocks for under $4,000.

Not a bad day's work, all in all. You set the stocks aside and forget about them as the recession draws to a close. Somehow Fannie Mae has managed to weather the recession, and because of it your

How to Get Rich during a Recession

stocks rise in value back to their original price of $16 apiece. That means that the stocks you purchased during the recession, the ones that you paid less than a dollar for, are now worth sixteen times their original value. That means that instead of the $4,000 worth of stock you thought you had, you're now sitting on $64,000 worth of stock.

That's a $60,000 gain. $60,000, a year's worth of salary for part of America's citizens (two years' worth for many) to get you started in your new life, all because you had the good sense to invest in the stock market when the selling price was low and the stocks were being agreeable. You saw the opportunity and you took it, and now you're going to reap the rewards.

Chapter 3- How Employees Can Be Recession-Proof

There are many ways to use an economic recession to improve your future and reap a profit; however, most of these methods require you to take a long term view on the effects of the recession, and to sit back and allow the poor economy to roll right over you. That's a great attitude to take if you have hundreds of thousands of dollars sitting in the bank and can afford to wait the economy out; however, if you're like most of the rest of us you're operating on a tight budget even when the economy is booming!

If you're barely getting by when the economy is good, how on earth are you going to manage to keep your head above water when recession is flooding businesses from coast to coast? It can be done, if you're smart enough and savvy enough to look for the hidden opportunities hiding behind every misfortune.

Recession-Proofing Your Job

The first thing you want to do is protect your job. As I mentioned earlier, it's going to be the small start-up companies who haven't firmly embedded themselves into society that will feel the ax the fastest when a recession comes around. When people stop spending money, they're going to be among the first companies to stop receiving it because they simply haven't had time to dig in their roots.

If you work for a company that's going to feel very little effects as a result of a recession you have very little to worry about. Regardless of what company you work for, however, now is a great time to start making yourself indispensable. It's simple fact that the employees that are the first to go when a company starts making lay-offs are the ones who aren't deemed to be important enough to stay-sort of like acceptable loss in a war zone. Those employees have to go in order for the company to thrive.

Making yourself an indispensable part of your company is the first step toward recession proofing your job. Even companies that are cutting down on their staff are going to hesitate to get rid of individuals who are essential to their company's daily operations. This would be an excellent time to consider volunteering to take on extra work or become more actively involved in long term projects or contracts.

If you can, involve yourself in several projects your company is working on (obviously without stretching yourself so thin that you can no longer do your job to the best of your ability). The more pies you have your fingers in, the more hesitant management will be to let you go. In times of recession companies may be cutting back on their employees, but that doesn't mean that they're going to be able to cut back on the amount of work they have to do. It just means that that work is going to be re-delegated. If you're already actively involved in several ongoing projects the company will find it much easier to simply accord you extra responsibilities on these projects than to attempt to bring a new man up to speed.

A heads up-this is NOT the time to attempt to apply for a promotion or a transfer, however promising that transfer may be. The minute you accept this type of move you become the new man on the block, and immediately become more vulnerable when the time comes to go through and decide who will go and who will stay. Right before the string of layoffs in 2007 due to the termination of numerous government contracts one well known government agency had just opened a new department and moved a large quantity of their oldest and most experienced employees on over. Despite the fact that many of these employees had put in more time with the company than the management they were working under, because their department was "new" they were among the first to lose their jobs when the company started laying off.

Attitude counts-a LOT. A recent article published by Fortune magazine stated that when management is trying to decide who will stay and who will go, often attitude and the employee's ability to boost morale is as strong a determining factor as their ability to do their job. When the going gets tough, the tough have to get going. Remember, companies trying to stay on top during a recession are going to have higher expectations of their employees than ever before. The only way these employees are going to be able to meet those expectations is if they are able to keep their morale high.

An employee who drags that morale down is going to quickly find themselves looking for another job.

Just in Case...

Hopefully the economic recession isn't going to impact your job- but that doesn't mean you shouldn't take precautions. You don't want to wait until you're holding your pink slip in hand and wondering how you're going to make next month's mortgage payment to start looking around for another job, and you don't want to wait until you need something from them to touch base with your old bosses and co-workers and your friends and acquaintances that might be able to offer you work when the going gets rough.

Network

It's all about networking. If you know anything about real estate you know "location, location, location" is every agent's mantra. (Right after "Buy low and sell high".) A piece of property that's within easy walking distance to schools, grocery stores and public transportation is going to be far more desirable than one that is miles away from everything, no matter how beautiful the location.

The same thing applies to you when the time comes for you to find a job. That house in the middle of everything is going to sell much more quickly, and you, in the middle of a huge network of friends and potential employers, are going to be able to find work much more rapidly. If you've kept in touch with your bosses and associates, both past and present, you'll not only probably already know who's hiring and who's not, you may have the inside track when it comes to finding another job.

If you wait to get in touch with them until you've been laid off, however, you're going to find yourself struggling. They're going to know that the only reason you're contacting them is because you're hoping to get a job, and they're going to look at you unfavorably-not only because you're willing to use your friends that way in the first place, but that you would be caught so unprepared. They're going to be far more concerned with their own affairs at that point than they are about yours.

Be Visible

No matter how much you've been looking forward to spending the next three weeks onboard a Carnival cruise ship, when your company starts making budget cuts is absolutely, positively not the time to take an extended vacation. You can't show someone how valuable you are if you're not there! When they sit down to review employee records and someone asks, "Hey, where's…?" and someone else answers, "Oh, he's on vacation…"-well, you can imagine where that conversation is going to go.

That doesn't mean you have to deprive yourself of a well-earned week away from the office. If you tend to take your vacations in bulk (disappearing for two to three weeks at a time) this is a fine opportunity to spread those vacations out a little-a week here, three or four days there will give you a break while still keeping you in the corporate eye. No one expects you to work yourself to death (and if they do, they'll never admit it in public). You just don't want to take that vacation at a time when taking a little break could turn into an extended one-as in, permanently.

Remember, the average recession in the United States only lasts eleven months. Giving up your extended vacation for a single year is a small price to pay for keeping your job…and your paycheck...and your 401K...and your health insurance...You get the picture. You can always enjoy that month in Aruba next year.

Offer Suggestions on Ways to Save the Company Money

In the middle of a recession even companies that have historically been very employee oriented are going to have to shift their focus from creating a great place to work to creating a way to trim the fat off of their budget while continuing to remain competitive in the marketplace and lure in consumers who would otherwise prefer to spend their money elsewhere. This is going to be their top priority!

Because saving money while still continuing to make money is going to be a vital part of the company's continued existence (and because it can be so difficult to do in an economy that thrives on the idea that you have to spend money to make money) an employee that can help them achieve that goal is going to instantly become one of the company's greatest assets. You don't dispose of assets that are generating a tangible return in the middle of a recession. Employees that can help a company move forward while at the same time preserving their bottom line are going to be worth their weight in gold in the eyes of the corporate bigwigs, and you can guarantee that these individuals are not going to be the ones standing in the unemployment line!

Can't come up with any clever suggestions to help your company cut its costs? Here are some ideas to get you started:

- Trim the fat on the office supplies. You'd be amazed at what the average office spends in pencils, paper and folders a month!

- Find a way to go through and lower production costs without losing quality.

- If you can discover a way to decrease the cost of transporting your products you will instantly become your office's golden child! The increase in the cost of oil (and subsequently gasoline) has spurred an almost ludicrous increase in the cost of transporting goods, which in turn has forced companies to raise the price of their goods, which in turn is leading to the loss of business in the recessed economy as customers complain about the increase in the price of goods and take their business elsewhere.

- New employee perks. Companies that don't offer their employees any perks whatsoever usually don't have employees for very long. Even the most unconcerned companies generally host a Christmas party or other annual event for the people that keep the wheels of their company turning, as well as a steady stream of incentives throughout the year to keep morale high and encourage greater productivity. If you can think of a steady stream of employee (and client) perks that will require the company to part with less money out of pocket you will be well on your way to establishing yourself as an invaluable member of your company's team.

Keep Your Skills Up-to-Date

It doesn't matter what industry you happen to be in, sweeping changes in supply, demand and technology are going to require you to stay up to date with what's happening in the field. If you've simply coasted along up until this point, grandfathering your way along while your co-workers went back to school, attended certification classes and furthered their education, you're going to find yourself in a sticky situation in the middle of a recession.

When preparing to weather a recession companies are going to consider the long term outlook for their company rather than the short term, which means that their priority when considering which employees are going to go and which ones are going to stay is finding high quality workers that are going to be able to help the company keep pushing forward in changing times.

This is one of those times when that insignificant little piece of paper helps.

Unless you have worked extensively with the technologies or programs that your company specializes in and know it inside, outside and backwards without the benefit of taking a class or two to show you how to do it, you're going to find yourself pushed out of the way in favor of a younger employee who has taken the time to expand their horizons.

Education counts. If you haven't already, take this opportunity to see what kind of tuition reimbursement your company offers and what certifications are available in your field.

THERE IS NO POSSIBLE WAY TAKING THIS STEP WILL HURT YOU!

Ideally, furthering your education will make your boss see what a valuable asset you are to your company and keep your job secure during these trying times; however, if your company still decides to let you go these certifications are going to look great on a resume when you go to find another job. Companies love ambitious, motivated employees as much as they love well educated, experienced ones, and by taking the initiative and obtaining these certifications without any nudging from your boss you'll be proving yourself to be both.

Samantha Lee Bernard
Keep Looking

Walking around advertising the fact that you're looking for another job never endears you to employers, but covertly doing so in the face of an economic recession and a possible lay-off is just good sense. By continuing to job hunt even though you already have a job you'll be accomplishing several things:

- First and foremost, you'll be able to keep a weather eye on what's coming available on the market-and with whom. Although you don't want to be the new kid on the block when companies are looking to start cutting their payroll, if a favorable position becomes available with a company that stands a very good chance of weathering a recession while your company is almost guaranteed to cut your job in the next eight to twelve weeks, you'd be a fool not to snatch at the opportunity.

    It might mean taking a little bit of a chance, but the bottom line is that by doing so you'll also be setting yourself up to be gainfully employed while your co-workers are standing in the unemployment line.

- Secondly, you'll be preparing yourself for change. If you've ever seen the children's video Kung Fu Panda you'll remember the infamous words of the immortal Master Oogway-"There is no good news or bad news. There is only news." The determining factor in whether news is viewed as good or bad is precisely that- how you view it.

If you look at a recession and a possible layoff as a stimulus for change (change that you can be prepared for if you make the effort) then you will have no problem when it comes time to say goodbye to the old and hello to the new. On the other hand, if you're still rooted in the thought that the world is going to come to an end if you lose your job and have to go hunting for another one you're going to find yourself mired in confusion and misery when you're handed that pink slip-a mucky place that is going to hold on to you until the consequences become all too obvious.

What if You Get Laid Off?

"When one door closes, another opens; but we often look so long and so regretfully upon the closed door that we do not see the one which has opened for us." - Alexander Graham Bell

It started off as a regular morning. You got up, had your daily fix of caffeinated Columbian goodness, wolfed down a bagel sandwich from Dunkin Donuts on the road and strolled into your office with your briefcase in one hand and cell phone in the other-only to have the boss come by and tell you (without nearly enough regret) that you've been laid off and you only have two weeks to find another job.

Unfortunately, hundreds of people are going to find themselves in this position as the economy continues to take a downturn. No matter how normal it may be, an economic recession is going to take a toll on its residents. At this point, you're going to have two options. You can choose to flip your lid, like Milton in the movie Office Space, clinging desperately to your belief that the company could never really let you go because they can't possibly function without you. Or you can choose to sadly pack up your stapler, your calculator and your top secret stash of Werther's Originals that you've been hiding in your desk since last Christmas and move on.

Studies show that Generation X and Y'ers entering today's workplace have a far better chance of riding out an economic recession without suffering a major blow to their self-esteem or their financial security than the baby boomers. Why? This is because the thought of spending their entire adult lives working for the same company never occurred to them. They expect to switch jobs several times in their careers, hopping from opportunity to opportunity as it presented itself, and are more likely to look at a layoff as an opportunity to round out their resume in other areas than their older co-workers.

This is who you want to be. You want to be that employee that looks at that pink slip and thinks, "Hmmm, maybe I'll finally get the chance to try my hand at teaching college/coaching soccer/writing the next great American novel/etc." No, the next year might not help you make great strides toward who you want to be when you grow up. Yes, you might find yourself living hand to mouth for a couple of months while you adapt to a new lifestyle and wait for the chance to slip back into the industry you intend to call your own.

The point is, one way or another, this too shall pass. Sooner or later the economy is going to kick back up, and you'll be able to get on with the plans you had when you first took that job you were so worried about losing. The question is how do you intend to spend that time in between? Do you want to spend it constantly sweating and worrying about how the recession is going to affect your financial situation? Or do you want to be able to grab the opportunity presented to you with both hands and say "Not a single second of a single minute of a single hour of a single day passed be by that I wasn't looking for that open door!"

Chapter 4 - Recession-Proofing Your Business

If you're the owner of a business you're going to have a much more personal view of the effects of the economic recession, because it's going to be your profit margin that's beginning to show a loss. It's times like these when many business owners find themselves wishing that they could go back to the days of being a mere employee, because then all they had to worry about was whether or not they were going to keep their job-not whether or not their investment was about to come crashing down around their heads and leave them in debt and bankrupt.

The good news is that if you're a business owner facing the inevitability of an economic recession you're in a unique position to take advantage of it. An economic recession can be the savvy business owner's best friend if you know how to use the opportunities that only present themselves in times of hardship like these. If you're prepared to take the steps you need to take in order to make those opportunities a reality then you're in a perfect opportunity to ensure that when all those other businesses out there are floundering yours continues to thrive.

How Low Can You Go?

The first thing you have to remember is that an economic recession happens for a reason, and that reason is that people are trying to hold on to their money like they're afraid the next Great Depression is waiting right around the corner for them. You're not going to be able to pry that money out of your customers and clients with clever marketing strategies. They're far too clever for that (or so they would like you to think).

If you can't get money out of them the old fashioned way, how are you going to keep your business afloat? By doing what businessmen and women have been doing for centuries to make sure that they stay on the top of their game. You're going to undercut your competition!

Think of it this way. If you only had fifty dollars in your pocket and you needed to buy a new lamp from your home, where would you be more likely to go to purchase that lamp? To an expensive retailer that specializes in high quality lamps and might have something that was only a little scratched or chipped for fifty dollars or your local Wal-Mart, where you can purchase a perfectly fine lamp for half that amount that will be more than serviceable until you have the money to buy something high quality that will last?

How to Get Rich during a Recession

If you're looking at this and wondering why anyone would pass up the opportunity to get a once in a lifetime deal on a decent lamp you obviously haven't looked at Wal-Mart's financial reports lately. There's a reason that Wal-Mart is one of the top retailers in the country, and it's not because it offers high quality, one of a kind items. It's because it offers mediocre, generic but necessary items cheap.

Stores like Wal-Mart thrive in times of economic recession like this because even those shoppers who turned their nose up at the idea of shopping someplace so completely lacking in designer brand labels will view things a little differently when their budget doesn't allow for them to continue living the lavish lifestyle to which they've grown accustomed. They are thrust into a position where they will dominate the retail market because they are able to offer a wide variety of the basic and not so basic necessities of daily living (like living room lamps) at a price dramatically lower than that of their competitors.

You want to take a page out of Wal-Mart's book. During an economic recession people are looking for ways they can save money, even if it means accepting slightly inferior quality products and services. If you can offer them top of the line products and services for a lower price than your competition, you will have done three things:

1) Ensured that you have a steady stream of profit coming in at a time when most businesses are losing money. If you can convince these customers that you deserve to have their business you'll be able to keep money flowing steadily into your pocket-and you better believe they're going to tell their money-conscious friends.

2) Stolen them away from your competition. Loyalty is a beautiful thing in the business world. As a general rule, when consumers

find a provider or supplier that they are happy with they will continue to do business with them to continue enjoying that same smooth relationship...even if it means they have to spend a little extra.

An economic recession takes loyalty like that and throws it out the window, because when you get down to it most people are far more worried about the state of their own pocketbook than they are about whether or not a company they happen to do business with stays in business. If you can offer your goods and services at a lower price than your competition you can rest assured that you're going to be enjoying their business for a long time to come.

3) You've cemented your future. As I mentioned above, consumers develop an incredible sense of loyalty for the providers of their goods and services when the experience has been good. By stepping in and offering them a great deal you've laid the foundation for building a fantastic relationship with your customers, and while you continue to offer them that same great deal you're guaranteeing that even when the economy picks back up you'll keep their business and their loyalty.

Regardless of how dirty or underhanded it may feel take the time to shop around and see what your competition is charging-then deliberately undercut them. Remember, all's fair in love and war, and when it comes to helping your business through an economic recession it's definitely a war.

Keep Your Business Macro in Scope

The number one thing that the shift to e-commerce has taught us is that with the huge amount of competition we face out on the market, if we want to have a chance at succeeding we need to

How to Get Rich during a Recession

specialize. Tackling a large niche is simply too risky, and you're going to be facing so much competition that your consumers are going to walk away long before they know what you have to offer in favor of someone who clearly is going to be able to give them what they want.

An economic recession is the exception to the rule. During an economic recession people's primary motivation is going to be to save as much money as humanly possible, and while that recession is gradually weeding its way through your competition you want to be able to step in and pick up as many of the pieces as possible.

What am I talking about? Let's say that your business specializes in providing transportation services between the Greyhound station and the local universities of a major city. Good work if you can get it! Then an economic recession hits, and people are beginning to find it more economical to either walk or hop public transportation as opposed to maintaining and parking a car or calling a taxi.

Suddenly you're faced with a dilemma. There are literally hundreds of people every day leaving the Greyhound station for parts unknown in the city, and every one of those people needs a ride because they refuse to waste their precious money on private transportation. They're not all college students, however, and they're not going to be dependably heading between one university and another.

What do you do? Do you simply allow this opportunity to pass you by, or do you expand your horizons a little?

This is an excellent example of how an economic recession can help a business by subsequently driving to it a client base that it might not otherwise have had. There's very little chance that any of these people would have been interested in hopping a ride to the local university unless they were headed someplace nearby, but if you were willing to spread your wings a little bit and provide transportation to various points throughout the city rather than simply the universities you could potentially open the door to quadrupling your profit margin.

Your business will grow because it will become more macro, less specialized and more generalized in a nod to the need of the people around you. This is in direct opposition to what you've been told regarding the development of businesses in today's economy, but guess what?

A changing economy = A changing business

If your business is going to survive this recession without lifelong consequences it can only do so if it is willing to change and adapt. Do you remember when we mentioned earlier about the need to become more diverse and put your fingers in more pies in your company in order to recession proof your job? Just because the quantity of providers decreases during a recession doesn't mean that the need for the services go away.

In making your business more generalized you're only doing on a corporate schedule what others have done on a private one-you're generalizing and putting your fingers in more pies. A corporate accountant will stretch out to encompass the company's investments and serve as a personal financial counselor to the CEO to help the company take advantage of the opportunities offered by the stock market in light of the recession. A shuttle bus driver will extend their services to shuttle passengers all around the city.

It's all about becoming more macro and reaching out to markets that have previously been closed to you but which are now open due to a renewed need for the services you have to offer. The work

How to Get Rich during a Recession

is still there. The consumers are still there. The need is still there. The difference is that now you're going to be the one to ride in and scoop it up.

If you have any experience in investing you know that the key to successful investing is to maximize your profit margin (your ratio of cost to sale) as much as possible. In other words, you want to buy low and sell high!

An economic recession provides you with a unique opportunity to do that, but you have to be a savvy enough investor to know what to do with yourself when you're finished. One of the many downsides to an economic recession is that it inevitably causes the value of people's assets to drop dramatically. Houses that were worth hundreds of thousands of dollars the year before will be lucky to sell for six figures. Stock prices will be down fifty five percent.

This provides investors with the golden opportunity they've been looking for. As the recession drives the prices on these investments down lower than they'd ever go under normal circumstances investors are given the chance to swoop in like a knight in shining armor, scoop up these investments and then-wait.

The biggest boon when it comes to economic recessions and business is that although it may take a few months (or years), sooner or later the economy is going to rebound. When that happens, the value of all of those assets that weren't worth anything during the recession is going to increase as well. At that point you're going to be sitting on a gold mine!

Samantha Lee Bernard
Open Yourself Up to the Possibility of an International Market

Prior to the advent and mass popularity of the Internet, engaging in international commerce was a huge and difficult proposition that required you to be able to vastly undercut their domestic suppliers, provide your own means of communication and transport of your product, and most importantly, develop the right network of contacts to open doors to an industry community that will allow you to justify the investment of exporting your goods and services overseas.

And, of course, because the American economy placed such a high value on the U.S. dollar you had to convince these companies that they were justified in paying a higher price for your services than they would if they simple worked within their own borders-or at least their own continent.

There have been several events that have changed this, and which have made opening your doors to an international community not just a desirable move but a necessary one. First and foremost, the Internet has connected companies all around the globe into a single network of industry providers. Once upon a time it was inconceivable that a company in the United States would be able to write a computer program for a company in Beijing and have it in their hands by suppertime. The Internet has made that possible. It has also made operating in an international community more lucrative and cost efficient than ever before.

Unfortunately, the recessed economy in the U.S. has caused the relative value of the dollar to drop dramatically. Believe it or not, when you're considering opening your doors to the international community this is actually going to work in your favor!

How to Get Rich during a Recession

A large part of the reason for the huge quantity of layoffs in the United States since the beginning of the recession is that U.S. companies have discovered a cheap labor base in companies overseas with a weaker economy. a company choosing to outsource its customer service support to the Philippines, for example, will pay those workers less than half of the minimum wage required by the U.S. government-and realistically, how many Americans are going to be willing to put in the time and effort required to succeed in corporate America for minimum wage in the first place?

These employees don't have to be paid vacation, or insurance, or retirement, or any of the other "perks" that companies are offering American workers in order to ensure their loyalty and services rather than losing them to another company that's willing to provide them with that. Because of it companies are able to cut the costs of their payroll dramatically. When the company is already suffering from a reduction in profits due to an economic recession, saving those expenditures looks pretty good on their bottom line.

You can make that same principle work for you. With the value of the dollar falling there is no longer such a dramatic difference between our pay rates and the rest of the world-and if you can take that reduced dollar value and combine it with the ability to offer your customers and clients a great deal on your goods and services you can place yourself in a position not just to be able to justify your services, but to give your clients a reason to prefer them.

Top quality work at a bargain price!

Chapter 5 - Unbelievable Benefits of Recession

Economic recessions are a vital part of the economy, and they can play a huge role in helping you and your company look forward to a bright new future. These aren't the only benefits of a recession though! Now that the heavy-duty stuff is out of the way, let's take a second to look at some of the lighter benefits of a recession-the little day to day perks that will help you get through until the investment of your time and your money and your willingness to take the long term view pay off and you're able to enjoy everything that recession has to offer.

How to Get Rich during a Recession
Riding in Style has Never Been So Easy

In Part I we talked about how the real estate market responded to recession, and how the freefalling values of the housing market presented investors with real promise. The good news is that stocks and houses aren't the only things that tend to freefall in value when a recession happens!

If you've been holding out on buying that convertible or SUV of your dreams, now is the time to do it. Along with houses, cars are selling for pennies on the dollar what you would have paid for them before the recession. This is especially true of luxury vehicles, vehicles with poor gas mileage or other cars that simply aren't considered to be high quality commuting vehicles. These vehicles are so unpopular that they're sitting around on lots right now gathering dust and waiting for someone to come take them home.

Someone like you, perhaps?

I'll bet you never actually imagined that an economic recession could help you fulfill your dreams, did you? That's just another of the hidden benefits of recession that no one talks about because they're so busy hemming and hawing over the downsides. The simple fact of the matter is that an economic recession starts driving the prices back down of everything whose prices have been going up in the last few years in the face of an economic boom-and if you happened to take into consideration the fact that the price of gas is driving people to purchase small, functional commuting vehicles rather than luxury models or SUV gas guzzlers you find yourself with another golden opportunity staring you right in the face.

For example, a used car lot somewhere out west recently posted on its website the SUVs that had been sitting on their lots for an extended period of time. These SUVs had originally sold for $25,000 (ish). They were now on sale for under $16,000 and still gathering dust. You can only imagine what they will eventually sell for as the economy continues to fall. Imagine being able to purchase an SUV that once upon a time would have sunk you far into debt for less than 50% of their original value.

How can you argue with that?

You Can Find Anything Secondhand-Cheap

When people are trying to save money rather than spend it they're also trying to earn it, which means that secondhand sales abound. (Coincidentally, an economic recession is also a great time to be a pawnbroker.) If you're looking for something, chances are good that somewhere out there someone is selling it. That encompasses everything from socks to hardware to little red wagons and back again. This is a prime time to take advantage of the number of secondhand opportunities that are going to be available and do some things that you've been putting off for a while now.

What can you find secondhand? Virtually everything. Somehow, no matter how odd an object is there is inevitably someone somewhere who considered it to be an equally good investment, and now with an economic recession staring them in the face the need to get rid of the objects in question is almost overwhelming. That means that regardless of what you're looking for, between the multitude of Goodwill, Salvation Army and consignment shops that about from coast to coast, it is bound to exist somewhere.

Chapter 6 – How to Build Wealth in a Failing Economy

Let's talk about how we can get instant fast cash.

The key is to leverage on other people's resources:

- Leveraging on their massive traffic

- Existing buyer's needs

- Free Search Engine traffic like Google

- Or even selling free stuff for good price (high value involved)

There are a few ways you can look for fast cash. You can make money through affiliate marketing or AdSense, but you must have traffic to come to your site. Since buying traffic is not really an option, your best bet is to leverage on Web 2.0 sites, article directories, press releases, blogs or forums to get those visitors to come to your website.

There are many degrees of buyers as well. There are people who are already pre-sold on the value of the product and there are others who are not in that category.

The goal is to go for these types of 'low-hanging fruit' because they are the easiest customers to 'close'. In fact, they are probably ready to buy with credit card (or PayPal account ready) in hand; it is just a matter of whether you are the affiliate credited for the sale or if it goes to someone else.

So you might as well be the one to cash in.

Google is also a very good place to get traffic. Using Social Bookmarking, you shouldn't have a problem getting ranked on lower competitive keywords – for example, if you write a review on Squidoo or Hub Pages, you can leverage on their 'rank authority' and get listed on Google.

Lastly, there are many products with Master Resell Rights of Private Label Rights available on the Internet.

There are many places where you can easily and quickly obtain a large collection of products with Master Resell Rights or Private Label Rights. All you need to do is to look for these products on popular Internet marketing blogs or newsletters by subscribing to them.

You can easily make use of these products (they can be obtained at a relatively cheap price) and you can sell them off for a hefty profit.

All you have to remember is this – you have all the resources you will ever need to produce fast cash, so do not worry about a lack of resources.

How to Get Rich during a Recession
Handy Tools to Riches

All you need to do is go to Clickbank or Pay Dot Com and get started by promoting a digital product.

As I've mentioned above, Squidoo or Hub Pages are your best bets to serve as the platform for reviewing products that you can promote as an affiliate for fast commissions.

Other tools that you will need are a self-hosted WordPress blog (or a free BlogSpot blog if you don't have one).

Sell Your Skills

One of the fastest ways you can make fast money is by selling skills and services.

Can you do the following?

- Write articles

- Create beautiful graphics

- Debug or install a software or script

- Speak with an audible voice

- Even something as simple as submitting articles to article directories or comment on other people's blogs?

Let me tell you this – you can easily trade your skills for big money, especially if you are staying outside the U.S. and the currency conversion rate works to your favor. (Yes, even submitting articles for people or doing simple SEO work can be a very good way to get fast cash).

I've personally made tens of thousands of dollars just by providing writing services to people and it has single handedly funded my Internet marketing business while I was building it up. Today, I do not write as much but I outsource a lot of writing to other people thanks to my established Internet marketing business.

All you need to do is go to where the clients are!

The first thing you must do is to create your own account or sign up as a member on these sites. You will need these accounts to apply for projects there.

By going to those sites will teach you how to create your own account there. You can post or bids for jobs while you are there.

Bear in mind, when you are just starting out, nobody knows who you are so you will have to earn people's trust. The fastest way to get noticed is to show good samples of what you are capable of and bid really, really low. You will get offers or opportunities if they see value in your work.

Make sure you bid for as many projects as you can. The biggest pitfall would be to bid for 2 or 3 projects and sit there and wait. If you are really desperate for money, make sure you bid for every single project you are capable of (if you can handle all of them).

Now, someone may ask…

"What if I have none of the skills and services listed above?"

Good question!

How to Get Rich during a Recession

As a matter of fact, you can bid more jobs than you can handle and OUTSOURCE these jobs to other freelancers!

In other words, you the MIDDLE-man by bidding for projects and outsourcing to others even if you are not good at the skill or you are not willing to spend time working on it.

You can either outsource to other freelancing agents, or to people that you may know around your location. Preferably, it is better to go for someone you trust. The key to getting projects done is to consistently bid and outsource to the same person without telling them where you get the job (that way you can keep your profit margins higher.)

Increase Your Site's Traffic

I will share with you 4 strategies to get fast traffic to your website and make money via affiliate marketing or AdSense:

Social Bookmarking

Social Bookmarking is one of the easiest ways to get fast and instant traffic to your website. This strategy is quite viable because there are millions of visitors visiting those pages on a daily basis. Sometimes, they even send out newsletters to recycle the traffic. Either way, it is one of the easiest ways to get people to come to your site.

Article Directory Submission

Writing articles and submitting them to directories is a very easy way to get targeted traffic and increase your search engine rankings.

You can write a review and place your affiliate link on a Squidoo or Hub Page and drive traffic using a combination of Social Bookmarking and article directory submission. As long as you use a proper anchor text for your keyword you will be able to rank for certain terms easily.

A good example of using anchor text is to link a keyword like "Fat Loss 4 Idiots" rather than http://www.fatloss4idiots.com in the author bio box.

If you can't or won't write articles, you can always go back to those freelancer sites and get people to write articles for you for as low as $2 per original article or $1 to rewrite an article (some might even bid for half of that amount).

Submit Press Releases

A press release is like a news center where it publishes the latest news.

Comment on Other People's Blogs

One of the easiest ways to get fast traffic is to comment on other people's blogs.

Of course, you must make sure you do the following:

- Choose high traffic blogs (e.g. John Chow, ShoeMoney, ProBlogger, etc.)

- Make sure you are one of the first few people to post the comment there.

Bear in mind, never, ever spam your comments. Don't write one liners like "Good Post", or "Nice Blog"... make sure you post something constructive.

Cash in on Blogs

If you have a blog somewhere and it is rotting in cyberspace, then I strongly suggest you start monetizing them with the following strategies:

Getting Paid To Write Posts

Here are a few sites you can get a free account and start getting paid to write blog posts such as paid or sponsored reviews:

- Sponsored Reviews

- Pay per Post

- Review Me

- Blogvertise

- Smorty

The key is to bid for relevant topics on your blog and you can get paid anywhere from $5 up to $50.

Getting Paid To Publish Links

As long as you are willing to display links and send link juice (Do-Follow links) to other people's sites, there are companies that are willing to pay you for placing links up.

Here are a few good places to sell links:

- Text Link Ads

- Blog Rolled

- Kontera

Become a Guest Blogger

Another good way to get fast cash is to blog on other people's blogs. If they are offering opportunities, you will be able to get some exposure and money to pay the bills while you are building your very own blog.

Run a Fire Sale and Giveaway Event

A Fire Sale is a very good example of how you can gain very fast cash by pooling together a bunch of valuable products and selling them way below the normal price for a limited time only.

Vince Tan, a World Internet Summit (WIS) speaker has launched the biggest fire sale in the world, in an attempt to make more than 7-figures worth of sales without putting down a cent in terms of investment. This is just an example of using a fire sale concept to raise fast money (and big money as well).

Here is how you can run your own fire sale easily:

- First gather a bunch of useful products with Master Resell Rights or Private Label Rights (make sure you check the terms and conditions carefully to see if they can be bundled and resold or not...)

- Compile them into a package – preferably a good theme or have a good reason to run one (maybe you can call it a recession fire sale)

- You don't need to be a genius in copywriting, just swipe (not plagiarize) a good headline and change it to suit your own style. Place the product pictures one by one and you will have a sales letter ready.

- Invite a few JV partners to promote your fire sale. Even if you don't have a mailing list, you can ask your JV partners to contribute their products and link them to their landing pages. That way you kill two birds in one stone – gathering more JV partners and getting them to contribute products to your fire sale. A Sweet deal indeed.

- Sell for a very limited time using the scarcity factor and watch the sales roll it.

- You can try not to end the fire sale as well. Just keep them ongoing but raise the price a little to be fair to those who bought during the introductory or launch period.

Giveaway Event

Here is another good example of a perfectly executed Giveaway Event.

A Giveaway is an event where people get together and contribute gifts, and everyone works together to drive traffic thus sharing and building each other's mailing list in the process. Not only this a good list building exercise, you can also earn some profits while the traffic is still fresh.

Samantha Lee Bernard
Basically what you will need is a good theme once again.

Invite partners to contribute gifts and make sure everyone drives traffic to the site.

If you are the host of a giveaway, you will have lots of advantages because you usually are the one who gets the most leads or be the first to get traffic.

Once they have opted-in to receive your gift, you must make sure that you lead them to a good one time offer (OTO) page and sell them a product there. In addition to that you can also install a tell-a-friend script to get them to spread the word about your gift.

ABOUT THE AUTHOR

Samantha Lee Bernard is a financial adviser with a background in economics. She graduated cum laude at MIT and is currently working as a consultant for financial management firms.

Sam is a mother of five and a loving wife to Jack. In between her career and home life, she does yoga and is a very good cook.

www.ingramcontent.com/pod-product-compliance
Lightning Source LLC
Chambersburg PA
CBHW070831220526
45466CB00002B/795